My name is Anna, and I want to be a doctor like my Aunt Maria when I grow up. But first, I need to learn about my body.

I'll start with my new kitten, Jasmine. She doesn't look very much like me. But some of our body parts are the same.

I look into Jasmine's eyes and ears and mouth. She uses her eyes to see and her ears to hear, just like I do. I can see into Jasmine's mouth when she yawns. She has sharp teeth for hunting.

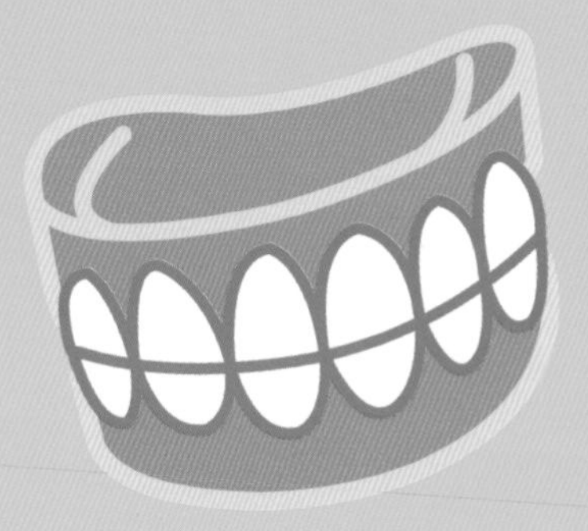

Ourselves

All About Me

Written by Lisa Bullard • Illustrated by Brandon Reibeling

Raintree is an imprint of Capstone Global Library Limited, a company incorporated in England and Wales having its registered office at 264 Banbury Road, Oxford, OX2 7DY – Registered company number: 6695582

www.raintree.co.uk
myorders@raintree.co.uk

ISBN 978 1 3982 3844 2

Printed and bound in China.

British Library Cataloguing in Publication Data
A full catalogue record for this book is available from the British Library.

Aunt Maria says I'm even more like Jasmine on the inside. Hidden bones hold us up. The bones are hard and protect the soft parts of our bodies.

A person has more than 200 bones in total.

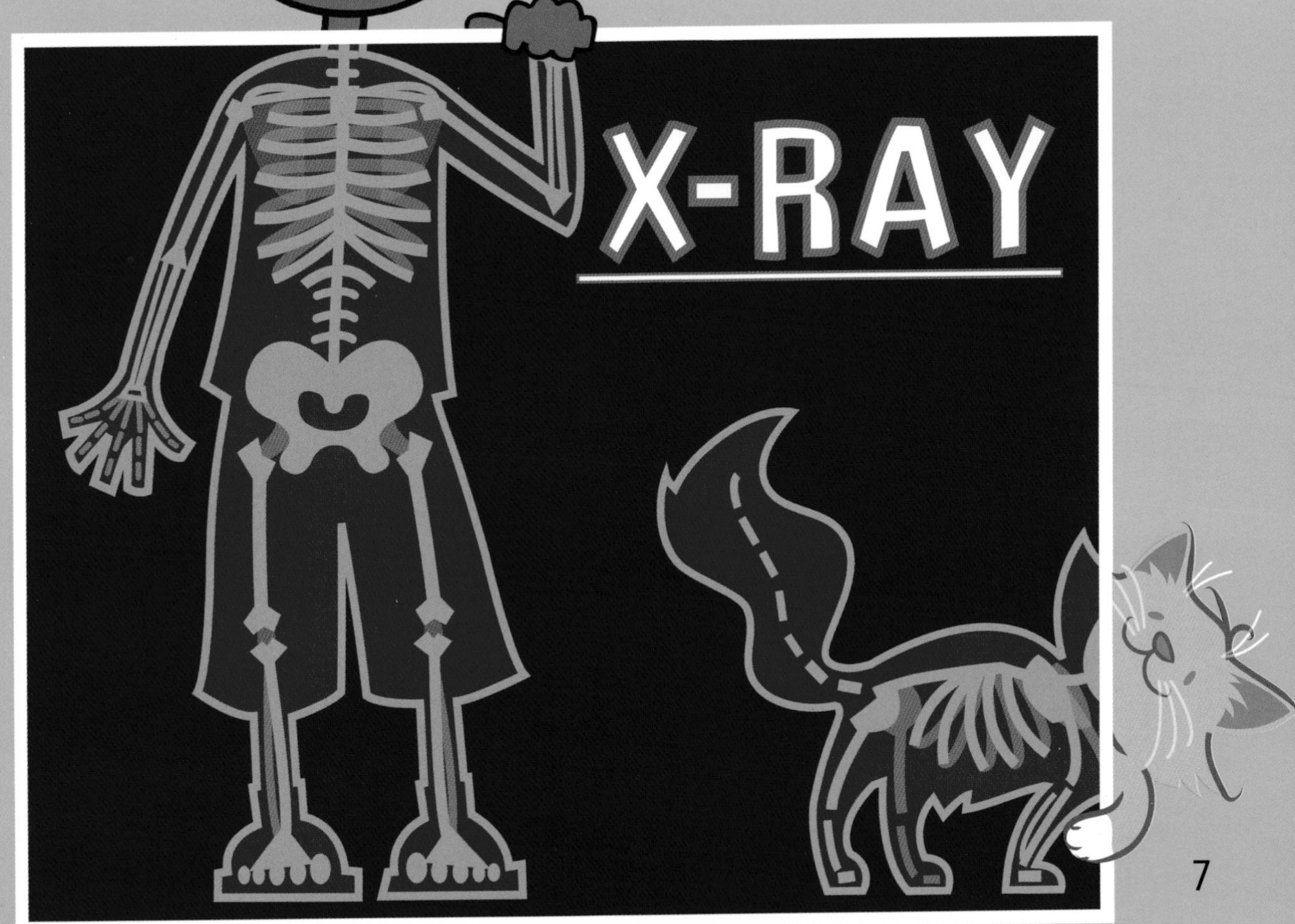
X-RAY

Muscles are attached to the bones. Muscles need exercise to make them stronger. Aunt Maria calls muscles our "movers and shakers".

I know what she means. My muscles always want to move, especially when I'm supposed to sit still.

Aunt Maria says the heart is one of our most important muscles.

She lets me use her stethoscope to listen to Jasmine's heart thumping inside her chest. It's pumping blood all through her body.

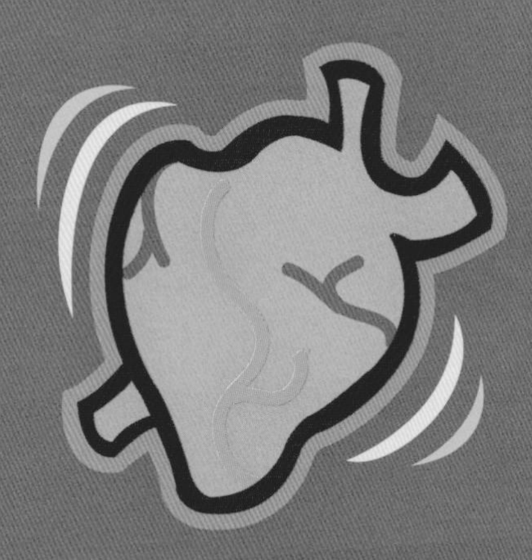

I listen to Jasmine's lungs, too. Lungs help us to breathe in the air our bodies need. Then we breathe out the used-up air. Jasmine breathes out cat-food breath!

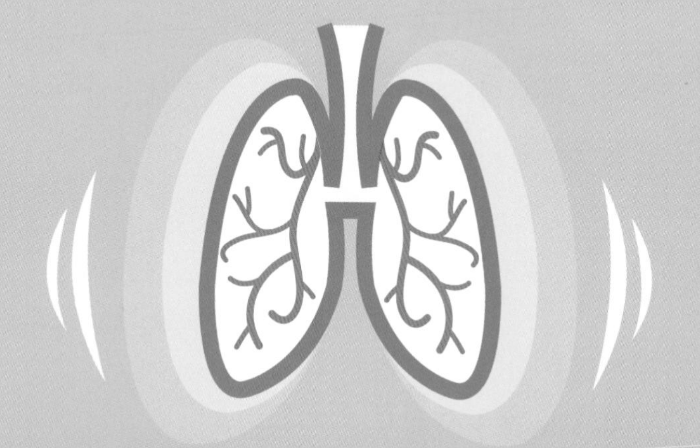

Aunt Maria says air goes down one tube to our lungs. Food goes down a different tube to the stomach. The good parts of food end up in our blood. The rest comes out as waste.

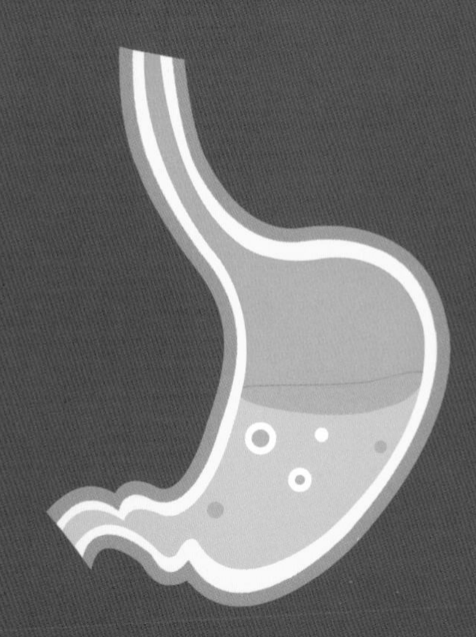

I don't know how lungs and a stomach and a heart all fit inside a small body like Jasmine's. Aunt Maria says that skin holds them in. Skin also gives hair a place to grow.

Skin and hair can make people look different. Angela has long, straight hair, and Kate just wouldn't seem like Kate without her red hair and freckles.

My new baby brother, Daniel, has no hair at all. Mum says he'll grow some soon. Even though Daniel's tiny now, one day he'll grow into a tall, strong man like Dad.

I asked Aunt Maria how our bodies know how to grow. She said that the brain is in charge. It tells all the other parts what to do.

Our brains also help us to learn. Aunt Maria says I need to study hard if I want to be a real doctor one day. Until then, I'll take good care of Jasmine.

Getting to know your body

Activity 1: Breathing and exercise

1. Stand still, with your arms at your sides. Pay attention to your breathing. Is it loud or quiet? Fast or slow?

2. Set a timer or stopwatch for two minutes. Jog on the spot until the time is up. Stop and listen to your breathing again. How is it different?

Activity 2: Self-portrait

1. Find a tall mirror and look at yourself in it. Think about all the parts that make up your body. Which parts can you see? Which parts are hidden under your skin?

2. Get a big sheet of paper that is large enough to fit your whole body when you lie down on it.

3. Draw an outline of your body. It will work best to have a friend trace around you while you lie on the paper.

4. Once the outline of your body is drawn on the paper, draw all of the parts of your body that you can see. Remember to add parts such as toenails and eyelashes. Then draw all of the parts that are hidden by your skin. Can you think of any parts that were not in Anna's story?

Glossary

blood a red liquid that travels through small tubes to every part of the body

bones hard parts in the body that protect the softer parts of the body and give the body structure

brain a body part inside the head that tells the body what to do. The brain also helps you learn and remember things.

heart a body part that pumps blood through the body to the other parts

lungs two balloon-like body parts in the chest that hold and use the air that you breathe

muscles stretchy body parts that are attached to the bones. They allow your body to move.

skin a thin covering on the body that holds muscles in place and gives hair a place to grow

stethoscope a tool a doctor uses to listen to your heart and lungs

stomach a body part that takes in food and helps break food down so your body can use it

Find out more

Books

Care for Your Body (Health and My Body), Martha E. Rustad (Raintree, 2022)

Lots of Things to Know About Your Body, Sarah Hull (Usborne, 2022)

Stop the Germs! (Health and My Body), Mari Schuh (Raintree, 2021)

Websites

BBC Bitesize: All About Me
www.bbc.co.uk/bitesize/topics/zqbxqfr

KidsHealth: How the Body Works
kidshealth.org/en/kids/center/htbw-main-page.html